# LAST APPLES
## OF LATE EMPIRES

*poems*

JESSICA LAMB

Cover art *Stewardship III* by Greg Mort (gregmort.com)
Design by Cheryl McLean
Author photo by Richard Sutliff

PO Box 434
Monmouth, Oregon 97361
www.airliepress.org

Library of Congress Control Number: 2008940512

Printed in the United States of America.

*for my mother, in the palm of one hand*
*for my grandmother, in the other*

Everything is plundered, betrayed, sold,
Death's great black wing scrapes the air,
Misery gnaws to the bone.
Why then do we not despair?

By day, from the surrounding woods,
cherries blow summer into town;
at night the deep transparent skies
glitter with new galaxies.

And the miraculous comes so close
to the ruined, dirty houses—
something not known to anyone at all,
but wild in our breast for centuries.

*Anna Akhmatova*
*(tr. by Stanley Kunitz with Max Hayward)*

# CONTENTS

## I

## I I

# III

# IV

I

# THE VOYAGE OUT

Inside the cell of a stopped car
without a warning flare, she
comes unfastened from her life.
When the light turns he drives on as though
she is still the woman who rose
from his arms that morning, leaving
on the pillow a strand of silver hair.
It is late, the streets are empty.
The whole way home she is no one.
If he spoke she might come back
but he doesn't, satisfied
with the meal, the wine,
the thought of her beside him.
He pays the sitter, locks up the house,
looks in on their sleeping child. The moon
shines through a fog. *Come to bed*
he calls to her softly.
It seems a small thing
not being the woman she was; almost
forgivable, his never knowing.

# NIGHT FEEDING

### 1.

I don't recall how I came to this country
but what does it matter? I've borne
a son; this must be spring:
everywhere the sounds of thaw, under a shroud
of fog so dense breath's taken with the teeth.
All night I swim the fields listening for cries
leaving the house lit up should he return.
At the edge of the woods, slick with morning's
brightening ash, the fuselage of a jet suspended
from a broken tree, lacy bones of devoured birds.

### 2.

A tulip, purple-black, expiring on the sill
above the sink, petals enormously splayed.
My husband calls for a drink. I rinse a glass
carefully, the stigma's red so frankly
genital. A bead of juice collects
in the cleft, the anthers' six black fingers
dusted with dark seeds.
The third day the petals furl and crisp
but fixed like flags they don't fall.
The water thickens, begins to stink.
He wants me to make love to him
somehow. I'm listening to the hum of things:
water turning in a glass, tulip
bowing toward decay. Whatever I promised
I could not have promised this.

3.

On the third night the milk comes, streaming
over the bed to the floor where first a pond
forms, then an inland sea. He wakes me
with his fists, tense mouth rooting for the spout.
I see wings skimming the moonlit milkpond,
beaks sucking up my white blood. As he drinks
the sea keeps filling and filling. I dream I'm falling
asleep dreaming of falling asleep, and this way
my spirit slackens deeper and deeper, drifting
light as milkweed through the marsh reeds
until dawn when he wakes me again, hooks me
with his tongue and hangs on.

4.

The beach freezes and thaws. The woods
are a deathly still white-sheeted room ahum
with disembodied sounds: prowling
of tomcats, beaks hammering trunks,
the furtive hiss of smugglers passing along
the night's goods: last apples
of late empires. Across the border
small ravening lips take hold.

5.

Dusk. There is no suffering here.
Tulips hold the last light
in sprawling yellow cups.
From the kitchen the sound of
rinsing. Each bone settles
into its nest of muscle. The lungs
begin their night rounds
drawing the darkness in, then
doling it out again, warmed.

# PARTIAL ACTS

When I was fifteen, made of the finest
luck, my mother sewed me a dress
straight from a favorite painting.
As the scene re-opens I'm middle-aged,
wrapped in a faded robe in front of a dwindling
fire. The man of the house is out, our son's asleep.
An old flame of mine was here a moment ago;
we sat across from each other
sipping our favorite Fumé Blanc.
Now that he's gone off to carry on
his richly separate life, I'm left
staring at Kathleen Battle, reclining
on a dust jacket, wearing a color I never knew
existed, unmistakably the color of everything
I crave. She is wearing it as if it were hers alone.
When I slip her out of the sleeve she leaps
doomed, delirious, demented,
into Semele's aria: *No, no, I'll take no less
than everything in full excess.*
I listen as Zeus gives it to her
against his better judgment
and she burns to a crisp.
I make her sing it again and again.

# THE CLEARING

Of all the nerve
making music in an empty house.
No one can hear me but the dust.

■

Each night I wash a single bowl.
Each morning I forget. What is it
I'm supposed to know? Overnight
a hole has opened in the road.
At the edge of the field,
a boulder holds its seat in shade.
The raven takes leave
of its night branch in the pine.

■

Beyond reach my garden
erupts into bloom; longing floods me. Infinitely deep
the lake of joy, the lake of grief.

■

Rain at dusk; the long day's loneliness
widens and stills. Sleep comes and breathes
the whole length of my body, tracing
invisible affinities
beyond number and name.
In night's enormous mind I hold
the whole of calculus
and still there is room
for the moon.

# THE BRIEF VERSION

We stood in the middle of route 5 near midnight
just outside of West Burke and got to know each other.
*Do I know you? Aren't you All of the Above?*
*Yes Yes Yes Yes!* Then
we kissed. Crickets
new-mown hay dewy blacktop lips
lips tongue lips. That sufficed
for speech,

for years.

# NEWLYWEDS

The Etruscan man and wife recline
on the lid of their sarcophagus
his pelvis pressed between her buttocks
terra cotta bodies worn
smoother than flesh
and in their sleek seductive smiles
the only epitaph to those inside
reduced to dust
in the hurry to undress

# HOLOCENE DREAM

I lay in the crook of his arm
as he read on and on in lulling tones
till sleep eclipsed me wholly,
a gust of ether and a puff of ash
marking the place where I had drowsed
attending to prehistory. I slept through all the ages—
calamitous eruptions, apocalyptic floods,
several mass extinctions.
When I awoke it was autumn.
All the familiar furnishings were there:
garden crows haranguing a murderous cat,
Jurassic dump trucks rumbling past
brimful of igneous rock
bound for Fairway Meadows Estates,
smell of soggy arborvitae with a hint
of perfumed laundry soap
venting from the neighbor's dryer.
I remembered nothing of my dreams
nor did I recall what caused the living world
almost to end before I could come into it
to claim my share
or, given half a chance,
to claim more.

# PORTRAIT OF THE ARTIST, DROWNING

There were the years when out of loneliness
I did nothing but read. I read expectantly, as if
erudition were the principal requirement
for a life of momentous encounters,
and as I read I imagined my own extraordinary
future, packed with romantic scenes like this one
in which I'm standing lost in thought beside a
Florentine fountain, say—or better, at the end
of a pier, the Adriatic swathed in fog, when a brooding
masculine form materializes, and after several moments
of gazing deeply into each other's smoldering
eyes, we fall into a passionate
discussion of Joyce (having both recalled in the
same instant the business about disappointed
bridges in *Portrait of the Artist*) and finally we wind up
back at his place after cappuccino and a chapter of Svevo
in the white heat of a bibliophile's long-delayed
embrace.

It almost happened once. We met in early summer
floating on the C&O canal in separate skiffs
reading the same book—Virginia Woolf's
*Between the Acts.* Later when he showed me into his
bedroom the walls were covered with mirrors,
dozens of them, all elegantly framed
straight out of the novel, slicing our reflections
into shards. It was like an inside joke
among the three of us, Virginia, Armand, and me.
This was the moment I'd been reading up for.
It promised everything—brilliance, fame, the end
to isolation. I waited for his kiss all night
as he snored through private dreams.

Whenever I read now,
today for instance perusing *The Art of Drowning,*
I have to stop in the first stanza and run to my desk,
already forming a reply, hoping I can get it down
in time, that one of you through layers of fog and
heavy drapes and accidents of circumstance
will be the one to hear.

# ENDING WITH "RISEN"


Another morning has come, nothing more
remarkable scheduled to happen. I open my eyes
to behold the usual rain and huddled there before me
like a coven of tightlipped wallflowers my clothes
hang in their closet, slouching on plastic spines
in shades of navy, moss, and taupe
except that single frightening foray into

pale yellow. Forgive me;
I really should take you out more often,
to the symphony where you could practice
better posture, or down the street to fetch
the daily paper. Today we might even walk
as far as the pond, where the ducks fatten
on Wonder Bread and furiously multiply,
skirting the neighbor with Parkinson's
because we hate and who doesn't to see a body
wasted. We'll sweep on through the golf course
past the new manses gloaming on the green,
massive garages and master suites with colossal
walk-in closets, where today the masters have woken
to the usual rain and, giving no reason nor
asking for one, just risen.

# FINDING IS THE FIRST ACT

I remember his hand discovering my naked breast.
All day as I'm remembering my bare skin burns.
He whispered, *This is heaven*. So all the time
it's been here, I thought. Nothing to prove or earn.
We walked out across the fields
in mist so thick our footsteps vanished behind us
and under the veil in the drenched grass un-
dressed and lay with one another, ruining the webs.
When the sun broke through we saw our tracks
circling the field and there we were in the center
of the final circle and all I wanted was all
my hands held.

# OCTOBER'S GEOGRAPHIC

At day's end I come in from raking leaves
to find you sleeping in a chair. I gaze upon you
lingeringly, from the thin pulse in your ankle
to the shallow divot under your chin where a boy
whose name you've long forgotten stabbed
a pencil lead in second grade. That would have been
1960: you were waiting to grow up, I
to be born. A whole lifetime seemed an infinitely
generous allotment.
What are you dreaming now, your fluttering eyelids
faintly purple like the inside of a mollusk?
Standing before you I imagine my way beneath
the layers of your clothes: between the shoulder blades
a patch of silver hair grows like moongrass
whimsically sown. This much I think I know
though your dreams remain dark—you'll wake soon
and shuffle down the hall to bed, one arm
embracing a pillow, the other encircling the space
that's mine to rise and fill.

# BRIDAL

For months after, I dreamed the scene
at the altar over and over, breathlessly scrambling
into church naked having forgotten
everything—rings, flowers, veil, vows, each other's
names—and then to top it off the track lighting
would explode or the septic system overflow
to further underscore the hopeless imperfection
of all human invention.
Finally there came the night when I was carried
in a white casket down the aisle covered
head to toe with lilies-of-the-valley, an angel
singing, *You are sweet peace and tranquil rest*
while another recited, *In your repose I ground*
*my dreams, my hushed expectancy.*
The Reverend was about to pronounce us husband and wife
when a light flickered on behind my eyes and I knew
I hadn't yet succumbed, though this is how it's said
to happen, first the serene hallucinations
then the final yielding up of will.

# WALK BEFORE SLEEP

At twilight we strolled home, your small hand warm
in my hand, April air a mild fleece. The cottonwoods

soaked up the lingering light and spilled it over the path.
Dark forms, man or beast, drew close and passed

without event. You murmured you were feeling sad just then,
small hand enclasped in my hand. I understood

you didn't need to name a cause; you knew of none,
feelings simply come and go like hiccups, or hail:

just yesterday a sudden storm ripped the new leaves down
and after it was gone the sun shone.

We crossed the swollen creek. Seamlessly you shifted
to a cosmic line of questioning—*will the sun ever*

*run out, can it make you go blind, why is it always*
*leaving and coming back, coming back*

*and leaving?* I remember your first weeks
when you wouldn't sleep without my hands

holding your unfinished body. I'd wait until your breath
grew quiet as a pine's, then lift my hands a hair's

breadth—slowly, as slowly it seemed as geologic time—
and you'd startle awake, staring up at me,

this transient instant before my hands flew back
to reassure was all you knew of being

alone in your body. What can I teach you
except the half truth we're both alone?

That we are none of us alone you were born
knowing, and you may persuade me yet, as all of space

falls like a soft pelt around us, your small hand
held warm in my hand.

# MONDAY, WITHOUT MAKING

I hereby declare this a day in which nothing is to be made
or unmade. Let my fingers wait unfastened
for the broken radio to blink on: say

*night of shattered glass*, switch off.
Let the witch's hair bloom on the cherry.
Since this is a day without making or unmaking,
let the colorless moon simply settle, not like
any other thing; let the white cat slip into the wood
unseen. Let the broken radio blink on:

*blind spot* with Brahmin accent.
For Kabokov in his Palace of Projects
be this a day without making.

For Chihuly no marigold macchia set
with Kashmir green lip wraps today,
no repairing the broken radio that blinks on:

*What is the difference between a window and a
table?...What is the color of fire when you are inside it?*
This is a day without making; let it break open
unusable and blink on and on, unanswerable.

# DENIAL OF THE MINOR POET'S PETITION FOR A CHANGE IN STATURE

First of all, you sleep too much. You never suffer
bouts of insomnia, waking aghast in the soundless dark
in dread of your impending death. Furthermore
you hate to sit. To work you require pots of tea,
the right balance of heat and ventilation. Forget about writing
in late summer before breakfast on family holidays
and during the depths of winter. Moderation is your mantra:
hold the strong coffee the stiff drinks and more-than-modest
extremes of feeling. If you strive for anything at all
it's for happiness—and who wants to hear daily updates
from the land of the blissfully contented?
No one wants to know of your waking in a nest
of husband son and cat at eight this Monday morning,
breakfasting on fruits from the garden
then ambling to your desk to find a pink rose
fragrantly adrift in a porcelain bowl, a gift
from your lover, the afore-mentioned spouse,
to whom you remain monotonously faithful.
We want to hear of the secret monstrous desires
of domesticity, of the face you glimpsed for an instant
in the melon before slicing it open, the ripe
gutting sound of slaughter, intoxicating spice
of incipient mold. We want you to tell us
what happened last December, the garden buried in decay,

the days shrinking—hunger failure rot incessant rain.
But you can't seem to stop delighting in the minimal:
oh the gleam on the surfaces of things, oh the many
kinds of white, from pearl to Corinthian to buttercream!
I think it's fair to say you've lost your claim.
An hour squandered staring into the mouth
of a blossom, and now you're abandoning your desk
in pursuit of the perfect summer lunch: vine-ripened
tomatoes with basil and a smattering of olive oil.
Then you'll inevitably nap while the pink rose turns
to brown and another day is permitted to expire
quietly, without fervor or calamity.

[ II ]

# A FEW QUESTIONS
# BEFORE I CONTINUE

If this is my one life by which door do I enter?

If a life is the shortest distance
between two points what will happen
if I open all the doors at once?

Where am I going with this line of
unknowing?

Does every strand come eventually
unraveled?

Does every door end at the same pass?

Who is not coming to visit me and why?

How many ways are there of arriving?

Will the rain please *will the rain*
just hurry up and say whatever it has to say?

What if a piece is missing?

How does the wind choose?

When the waters have subsided what will I
have held?

And how is this finally discerned?

# AMARYLLIS

I brought it home to find a blossom
already come and gone in the dark box.
The petals were slippery and stank
but they were perfect: blood-red, curved
back so the singular yellow stigma
stood gracefully erect. To think

of how this flower made itself: surging
past the plastic seal, forcing its way
to the top of the box, where its last cells
burst forth in a bloom designed
to sit upon my table and appall.

# THE DOOR

He is three when a pox
takes over his body.
I cradle him loosely, humming.
He lifts his arms away from his
blistered chest, hands clasped
like a supplicant's, on his face
a look I have never seen before:
not merely sadness or hunger.
He is standing at the door
of his body, asking to be let out.
It is the look I must have had early in labor
when it dawned on me there would be
no bargains. I had no choice but to open
over a night and a day in agonizing increments,
letting him finally into the world.
I want to tell how I've come to believe
it's better to give in,
feeling the body's pain or pleasure fully,
but I'm dumb with a kind of pain
there is no wisdom for:
I sit here while his flesh is glazed
with flame, and there's nothing on earth
I can do but hold him as
lightly as possible, singing
until I come to the last song I know,
then leaping off still singing
far into the night
for the love of him I can't help.

# SAVED, I.

When Phillip died of heart failure
sledding down the gentlest of hills
behind the school, everyone was sad
but not too sad. He always was
the weakest one; he had to have known
his days were strictly numbered.
His parents too (we saw them come
to claim his pale body)
had to have suspected death would
shortly take him, that very morning even:
surely they kissed him twice
as he ran to catch the bus. In Mrs. Bona's class
we were learning mammals and reptiles,
vowels and consonants, odds and evens.
Everyone was sad but only some
were smart and strong and would be spared.

# SAVED, II.

When Margaret's house burned up
with little brothers in it
we watched from the classroom window
saw the smoke and her face
seeing the smoke and were silent
but not ashen as she was, not sobbing. We were
whole. It was Margaret who had rips in the knees
bruises on the arms, dark circles under her eyes.

No doubt she knew she was born to suffer. But just
to be safe, we would hate her.

# LAMENT

All that I have made sleeps around me
ignorant of any maker.
The son I gave name coughs and turns to the wall.
Tonight I appear in dreams he will not remember
come morning. In the match we left unfinished
his knight is poised to take my queen.
This is the thanks I get
for sculpting each piece lovingly.

Even this fire I kindled burns brighter
now that my eyes are closed.

# WHERE HE COMES FROM

As his skin yellows in the days
after his birth on my father's birthday
I imagine my father's body after death
his blood emptying as blood's filling my son
and I wish my father would die
I mean *die out*
his whole sad race cancelled
no one but this golden child
and his mother remaining.
A week after his birth when the cord
dries up and falls
I think of my father's body long dead
skin blackened around the bones
and I wash my son for the first time
then wash him again to be sure.
When his first milk-shit comes
yellow and sweet as though he's
eaten goldenrod, I imagine how the earth
will smell with the body
of my father mingled in it
not as sweet as my son's shit
not sweet, not foul
acrid, smoky, like pumice. When he asks
where he comes from I'll hand him
a fistful of soil.

# DIRECTIONS

You wrote them with a sweaty
trembling hand (we'd been dancing)
on a receipt for nails:

*Plainfield, take the middle road*
*past the wood pile*
*follow the grass track to the squash patch*
*look for raspberries*

This is how and where I came
to you at last. You placed a ripe
berry on my tongue then
took it back with yours.

# THE MOOSE

He never comes when I call.
I march to the woods in the fog
of the predawn, his visiting hour,
and when he isn't there I yell out,
*Come on! I've conquered fear!* and freeze,
trying to look vacant, a vessel
waiting to be filled. Nothing comes.
Not the panther who's extinct
nor the wild boar.
I'd settle for a rabbit or a deer,
a sign—warm scat—a sound.
Once in cave-dark woods in love
I heard a woman's voice burst into song.

I drive back to the city at night
through forests of pine. It's then he comes,
his brown bulk like a running tree.
He pauses a second in the headlights,
long enough to look like death, then
lopes off, leaving me surrounded—
the forests I thought I knew
never so empty of me,
so full of life.

# HOMECOMING

We are sitting on the front porch
watching the rain move over the mountains,
flashing; he is remembering the violent deaths
of wild animals. An antelope
ran headlong through his window once,
bled to death on the living room floor.
The stripped green of his gaze sharpens
with something akin to humor. *It happens
to any unprotected thing.
Nature's a bloodthirsty mother.*
He tells of leopard attacks on herds of gazelle,
of the constant stench of carrion,
the predatory birds. I am his daughter,

wearing ivory earrings made from his last kill;
for his son, he brought the tusk that ended his career.
Peace offerings. How his little ones have grown.
We notice the acuteness of his elbows,
the starved babble of his fingers,
imagine him in Africa, carving spearheads
from tusks, claiming tusks with spears.
We were babies when he left and have imagined him
in more unlikely places: on the moon, under the sea,
next door, silently scoping us out
from behind his various disguises.
Now he's wondering how long we mourned him
after his presumed death. I have shown him the garden
I staked out when I was old enough to know of loss.
He'd return, I thought, by the time the sweet peas
grew to my four-foot height.

They shot above my head and blossomed.
The lettuce loomed in stalks and went to seed.
Tomatoes, cucumbers, and carrots,
harvested and canned year after year,
*To eat if we're ever stranded here,*
Mother said in jest.

On the southern-facing hill
I planted apple trees and berries.

At thirteen I added asparagus, which ripened slowly
and would give him time. I was all grown
when it first bore.

As I stoop to cut a few spears for his
homecoming feast, he wants to know how Mother died.
*It happened in her sleep,* I answer. *Aneurism.*
After a pause he says steadily,
*I like to think of death as a kind of detour.*
*To stay on course is an impossible feat.*
Yes, I consider responding,
there were times when I too could have disappeared.
Podding peas on the front porch while the men
set fire to the charcoal, I watch our piece of road
pressed into the wilderness, as familiar
as the press of my own lips against each other,

and I remember winters when a long, frostbitten
stillness seemed to stretch as far as foreign countries
from my window; the day my brother and I set out
toward town on skis, emerging terrified at dusk
in a valley ten miles from home,
too exhausted to breathe relief.
I am ashamed that Father found us
waiting, married to the same land
he left, marooned there.

We sit down to eat, hands clean, linen
in our laps, and the long-awaited return
has grown already ordinary.
I had wanted to greet him fully grown
in the garden, or under the apple trees,
my lap full of fruit.
But it is an old man not a king come home.
He may think he has come full circle,
back to his point of departure.
But this territory can never be reclaimed.

# LAST WEEK

When she coaxed us down
to the beach in the dark
was I the only one afraid?
The waves were fierce, her cancer
indiscriminate; this month's tide
the rare one known as syzygy, when the sea
recedes so far the beach ended and we
traipsed along the ocean floor.
Sparks trembled through the shallows.
Above us, noctilucent clouds, waning moon.
She told us about her journey
the places she'd been privileged to travel
the good people she had come to know
because of illness. Just last week
the telephone psychic had assured her
she would live. She was buoyant.
We followed her, warming—she would live,
we would all live, right to the edge
of optimism, where we stood for a long time
staring the ocean down, never doubting,
until she was too tired to stand.

# MOTHER'S PERFUME

I never dreamed it came bottled.
I knew it only as her skin's own
sweet secretion, and when she went out nights
with darkened eyes and silver ornaments, the scent would seem
renewed, a sign of quickened life, unstoppered
joy. She'd kiss my cheeks, her musky
pheromone outlasting her

until the morning I woke to find her
vomiting into a pail.
She sent me outside where Husband the Second
was mowing the field, stopping for nothing—
rocks, stumps, small mammals.
The Gravely stalled. He swore
and beat it till it started up again.

She was sleeping when I crept back in.
Everything smelled of sick, her sweat
mixed with his, a stink like rotting onions
leaking from a bottle on the bureau.
I pulled the cork. She raised her head and
stared. Staring back, I knew
this liquid ounce I held was all she really was.
*You may keep it if you like*, she said
letting her head fall back again.

# STILL LIFE WITH RIVER

On the day of my death the world in which I have no part
collapses to a point.

■

No longer nomad, I settled under an old elm to raise
my only son. In late summer when wind rocked the tree
I gathered my family inside to drink glassfuls
of cool water. Sometimes it was clear, other times murky.

■

When he was born in the afternoon of my missing
father's birthday, a mourning dove landed on the windowsill.
Actually it may have been a pigeon.

■

As for the man I married, he saw me first. He danced like a marionette,
smiling broadly. The story took a turn.

■

Before that I always lost things, thinking I would go back for them,
though I was never able.

■

My favorite pastime: following streams into rivers.
When I tried to do this in the city the water ran underground and
vanished.

■

There was a first garden. I ought to have left it behind,
but I stayed to tend the asparagus.

■

On the old mahogany bed with its pineapple finials,
I read mythology by day. With the dark came nightmares
I couldn't wake from.

■

Always the going down into sleep was the worst,
like pulling earth over my head.

■

I was terrified of trees, their night wail: *alone, alone, alone.*

■

In the blue kitchen he told me to eat
my eggs so I'd grow strong, so strong I could hold
Mother in the palm of one hand,
Father in the other.

■

She coaxed me out of her, devouring
an entire chicken. He smoked a box
of cigars. Finally I relented: June, Los Angeles
before smog; there are worse places, and anyway
my time has finally come.

# MUSHROOM

This is how my flesh will feel
when I've been dead a day—
cold, all the follicles capped
with a sticky death sweat, a brown
resignation blocking the pores
and just beneath, the perfect
serenity of a cleared-out concert hall
the quiet of the emptied
lung.

# FIFTEEN

Nothing to do for this fever but fall hard
on each other's mouths, lying sprawled
under a spindly tree in a litter-strewn lot.
Once before I'd kissed and promptly died,
playing Desdemona. For the occasion
my mother had sewn a white nightgown
from an old tablecloth. That was theater
but this was some awful delerium, a desperate
fumbling with buttons and clasps, bright ache
and throb the bodily length of every nerve
until I finally dissolved, wanting and not
wanting to want, trying not to think
of my mother and the nightgown shroud.
A warm rain began gently falling.
There was not a thing not wildly blooming,
even the street steamed fragrantly, his pink
rumpled shirt gleamed. At my door
we swore off kissing and vowed to rise
in the first tremblings of dawn to drink
a cold glass of milk, not thinking not thinking
of nipples and lips. And we did and we
didn't. And with that little death
the curtains came down.

# BODIES OF WATER

Lovemaking for maybe the twentieth
time all told our torsos flaccid
in early summer slapping together
like water against wooden pilings
you parted your white teeth to loose
the cry of the loon
sad bird that seems to hate the sea
and need it too always crying out
with some unspecific want and I
having just drunk a full glass
sloshed a little when rocked
as dark water gently slapped the sides
of the dory we drifted in laughing
this hidden estuary's only traffic
waiting for the tide to take us out.

# BEGINNER'S LUCK

First night on the river, camped in a driving rain
at Horseshoe Bend, we introduce our son to cards.
In seconds he's soaked us for everything we have.

He hunches there, laying out his pairs like a rich man
counting his bullion. We play over and over for hours.
It's the kings he must have first—at every turn he asks

for kings, whether or not he holds one in his hand,
and soon they come to him, irresistible in their
trappings of power, bestowing every last of his

impassioned wishes: if he wants queens, then
queens he shall promptly acquire.
The next day we reach the canyon where we conceived

this boy, now busily gathering jacks,
a sheen of luck gracing his tender head
like a crown. We're about to remark that here

at this bend in the river a couple of years back he had
his humble beginnings, but he's just won another game
and even to us it's unthinkable. Unthinkable

how this very one arrived so sure of himself and his place.
How to begin to explain as we're drifting down toward
Blossom Bar, while he sorts his cards again and counts them,

there is this thing called luck that's given him
a few good hands, and not because it's what he deserves—
though he does, he does; even in losing, he will.

# VISITING HOUR

Beneath the kumquat and the trumpet vine
my grandmother leans to kiss me goodbye.
If I hugged her hard she'd pulverize; I clasp
her wisp of hand. She lingers near me

for a while. When our time is almost up she asks
*Was there something I was meant to learn?*
thinking of her father perhaps, miserable man
put a bullet in his head when she was three

or the husband who threw his things in a bag
and left one afternoon while she was out.
I ask if she thinks she'll meet her loved ones
when she goes. *Wouldn't that be awkward*

she gasps, and then the shuttle comes
and she affords me one more kiss, her last.

[ I I I ]

# THE CENTER GROTON RECORD

Carl Bradley who has been very ill
is slightly better.

Everett Chapman and wife
spent Sunday in Ledyard.

John Goss has been putting up ice
with a gang of thirty men. A year ago
he didn't put up any.

Lyman Gard is cutting about twenty cord
of wood on the Copp farm.

Mr. Carter is putting up a wood shed
west of his house.

The Norwich and Worcester RR Co. have
voted to extend their line to Groton—so look
out for the engine when the bell rings.

Judson Burrows is suffering from poor health.
Simeon Gallup has closed his singing school.

# NIGHT WOODS

As ferns finger the purpling dark
as the nipplewort feeds
its myriad young and the horsetail
dims its lucid wands
Mother hides the milk
in the spring at the edge of the woods
I grip her hand
thirsting swarms
gathering in the dark
to drink

# FIRST RAIN

Yellow plum in the path like a lost egg.
Being no one's mother this morning
I devour it as rain begins to fall.
Pockets filled with more than I
could ever need I dash my spoils home
listening as the parched earth drinks
and drinks. It isn't enough. The first rain of
autumn never is. Skin bruised, my plums
have turned a sickly brown by afternoon.
In no time my ravenous son
will appear at the door.

For all I claim as mine what more
will be asked of me?

# THE BATH

This is the shore of Lake Champlain
this is the boy whose name is
rose-hedged-field
in a language no one speaks anymore.
He is four and three quarters, this is November
dark is falling, we are going out
upon the icy waters, I am his mother
*this is my raft*
*this is your raft*, we're going out
into the deep alone
and since there is
a war happening
we will be killed by torpedoes. Now
we must say goodbye. The son
straightens up. He's set to go.
Only his mother cries
*Stay! We could help each other*
*we could eat roots*
*until the war ends*. He hesitates.
*OK, I will!* he shouts, leaping up
as another missile falls.

# MOTHER INTRODUCES EVIL

My son's just learned that Peter Rabbit's papa
was roasted in a pie, an atrocity I'd planned
to mumble past for years yet, or possibly
forever. My mother reads to the end
without flinching, her voice a soporific
singsong, pausing only for a sip
of Chardonnay then picking up
*Squirrel Nutkin*—no stopping her.
My son is rapt, his pastel universe
abruptly turned a brutal red. One of his eyes
looks terrified, the other feral. She goes on and
on: once there was a king who beheaded his wives,
stored them dripping in a dungeon wherein
the new wife wandered, just as the others
before her. And then there was the widow
who stuffed her murdered husband's head
in a pot, planted basil on top. As he rotted
she wept; the basil thrived on his rotting and her
weeping. Then came the witch who killed a little girl's
mother: there was no body to bury, the witch
took it over, wormed her way into the father's
bed. That summer, bleeding roses
grew in the garden. Something was terribly
terribly wrong. No one would say
how she began, how she might ever
end.

# THRENODY FOR THE DEAD CELL

Whenever I cut my hair I dream
my mother's drowned.
I watch her sink, black hair
streaming like sea grass all the way down.
She always dies no matter what the cut.
I always wake appalled at what I've done.

I let it grow to the waist where she admires it again,
takes the thick rope in her hands, washing it
in the sea till the crescents of dirt beneath her nails
dissolve. Then comes the combing:
it's not her fault she rips and tears my hair
is a rat's nest the braid she weaves
makes my head beat wild drum beats—
a summoning. I'm drawn away from her.

Terrifying the way the hair falls then.
My mother sinks into her element.
I dream I've cut the bonds of
grief. I wake grieving.

# RETROACTIVE EPITHALAMION

When friends married in the fifth year of drought
we gave them a succulent as a wedding gift
a homely yet resistant Zwartkop rose
which they vowed to cultivate faithfully
through famines, epidemics, wars, winters
under siege when the lemon tree is sacrificed
for fuel, summers when fire devours the dry hills,
followed by a deadly season of sheer monotony
the valley of death agape between.
For now there was only the drought
which didn't worry us much.
We sat on the sweltering deck and laughed as if
stricken with a dread disease, its early stages
distinguished by hilarity and vicious thirst,
feverishly passing a bottle from one to another,
emptying and refilling glass after glass.

# AS IT WAS GIVEN

Every afternoon while the other boys played
stickball in the park, Bill and his father and brothers
sang barbershop quartets. The signal to begin
was a resiny hum from the cellar, where
Dad stirred house paint for the next day's job.

Soon they'd be standing in a huddle
harmonizing; the old man would toss out a few
words to hang the music on, and before long
a sound would appear overhead,
the purest overtone, like—here Bill paused
in search of the right analogy—
like a golden donut.

That was how he grew up, listening
for the golden donut. It didn't matter
that no one else seemed to hear it thrumming.
Every so often, he says, it still hovers overhead
for an instant, singing or no singing, then
just as suddenly vanishes.

# A FEW MINUTES ON
# THE FRONT STOOP

*The Weekly World News* reports
a fallen angel was found unconscious
in a pigpen in Iowa, struck by lightning.
And a man ruined his flying carpet
by machine washing it.

*Thank God for the rain*, Myron says
walking past with his sheepdogs.
*Keeps the moss growing on our backs.*

An aphid crosses my page
dressed in this year's
hot new color.

A hummingbird
shakes the pink rose,
flees in a shower of petals.

Humble brown moth
sucks what nectar
a dandelion has to offer.

*I'm having a writing retreat,*
I explain to my neighbor. She offers her husband
in case I need to lift anything heavy.

# AFTER FEVER

Rain finally lets up. The neighborhood I lately inhabited
is blurry with plum blossoms. I choose the low road,
avoiding obligatory chit-chat. Not gone far when there's
Barb in orange boots shoveling compost into her garden.
*Getting a jump on,* she chirrups. Her son Nick has a new
kazoo. *Hi!* he yelps. *Blow in here! It makes a noise! You try it!*
Barb hands me a pod of dried seeds, *Remember last summer's
poppies?* as if I could forget a red that red. It doesn't kill me
to thank her, blowing once into Nick's kazoo.
*Bluebirds,* she calls after me, *yesterday, by the river!*
*Plant your seeds now!*

# GIVING THE ORDER

Friday night at the neighborhood grill, my son orders a blintz
instead of his usual burger, thrilled to distraction by the word's
quick sizzle of obscenity. Next to us a boy sits
across from his father. *What day of the week is this?* he asks,
lifting a glass to his milky lips. His father turns his full
attention to the question, as if the child had asked for a key
to the secret workings of Nature. *This is Friday*, he answers,
watching intently as his son nods, seems to understand,
takes up his glass again. I wait for him to add in patronizing tones
*Do you know what comes after*, or *Which letter does Friday begin with?*
but he refrains, taking a long draft of his beer.
His son crayons the placemat while mine smirks over his
blintz-inspired graffiti: *Your blintz is showing, my
blintz is bigger than your blintz.* And then the father says
*There's something I've been wanting to tell you*, his brow
deeply furrowed. *It's about the days of the week.* I can't help
wincing for this boy who's being shared. He goes on:
*After Friday comes Saturday. And after Saturday,
Sunday. Those two days are called the weekend*
(continuing smoothly, gaining wind); *Monday is the first day
of the work and school week. After Monday comes
Tuesday. After Tuesday*...and so it goes, with no apparent
rupture in the given order of things. My son, whose hunger
for actual food has now outlapped his appetite
for innuendo, grumbles *What's taking so long?*
and no sooner have the words left his mouth
than the blintzes descend, giddily syruped.
The boy looks up from his instruction and exclaims
*I want what he has*! and flustered, the father
hushes him, saying *Now it's your turn,
let's hear you say them.*

$$\left[\; I\, V \;\right]$$

# SMALL SIGNS

Left alone the world
reverts to a room

I sit in it
thinking about nothing
but how to become the door
the words enter
the window
words reveal

the ear
listening
for the way
trees become
trees and green
turns into green

■

Out the window
a cloud drifts slowly
like a whale returning
to its feeding grounds
in the blue dark
I can see its spine
reaching all the way
to the next town
where the head has already
arrived at the end
of a long migration

just as the moon
opens its cold
patient eye

■

On the roof
rain repeats itself
it keeps coming
down and down until even
the trees appear to liquify
Listening means bearing
more than I can bear and yet
more keeps coming
I open my mouth
to cry out and a cloud
of mold spores
floats from my lips
the only answer is
to love small
signs of life

# SEVEN DAYS

1.

Take right now for instance
sky clearing after rain
steam rising off the ferns
growing lushly in the field
where last month they lay
mown to the nibs
an ocean unreachable but near:

I am one of those
getting just what I want.

2.

In the space of a single afternoon
I have managed to accomplish
nothing of consequence.
Through the open door the faint smell of corn
on moldering sheaves.
There is nothing to keep me
from sitting here breathing it in so I do
along with a thrush's song and a child's distant cry
weightless rumors sifting down
the long spout of the windpipe
into my innermost body.

3.

Blue-indigo of early morning
lost to the heavy
grey of 8 o'clock

I sneeze once
into my empty tea cup
the kitten gallops off

The house floats loose
washed clean of sound
kitten returns heart slowed
bats my wriggling pen
pen of rumor, palm of torn paper
pen of blunder, hand of forgiveness
lead me past the fog carry me
into the grove so I may leave
this offering before I warm
my small cup and enter
the mysterious cloister
of a grapefruit.

4.

What do we have here
buttered toast with
squirrels rustling
in the cypress
a day no sooner

started than ending
have you learned nothing
from the crows?
hardly an hour goes
by without six alarms
but the wind
dusting a crumb
from the desk
the wind has maybe
taught you too well
on its way out the door.

5.

From this paper I write upon
how many removes is the skin
of my own parched hand?

What animates this hand
dry from spring digging?
The still small form of my son
how strong is it really,
how vital his vegetable heart
under its trellis of delicate
ribs?

Do we exceed the stuff of which
we are made to which we so
eagerly return?

6.

Morning, a cry in the blood
though nothing grows
(this from the liver).

The feet ask do they really belong
in this world
the heart answers you must
since you suffer.

Whatever will I feed
a whole city
the mouth wonders
Roads impassable
says the cortex
find alternate routes.

Deliver me
the blood cries
cut it out
says the liver
remember me
(bones)
as you rise.

7.

And so I have lasted
another winter.

Do not hold
it against me
darkness,
for I am still
your creature
though my
pitiable body
can't help itself
begging for always
more light
even up to the last
day's last hour.

# ACKNOWLEDGMENTS

Grateful acknowledgment is made to the editors of the journals in which the following poems have appeared, sometimes in slightly altered form, and to Caldera, for a winter retreat in the Cascades during which some of these poems were completed:

*Antioch Review*: "Denial of the Minor Poet's Petition for a Change in Stature," "Night Woods"
*Calyx*: "Beginner's Luck," "The Door"
*Carolina Quarterly*: "Bodies of Water"
*Fireweed*: "Directions," "The Moose"
*Hiram Poetry Review*: "Bridal"
*The Laurel Review*: "Mushroom"
*Lullwater Review*: "Amaryllis," "Threnody for the Dead Cell"
*Mockingbird*: "Newlyweds"
*The Southern Review*: "Partial Acts," "Portrait of the Artist, Drowning" (previously titled "The Second Life of Art")
*Willow Springs*: "Night Feeding" (section 2, previously titled "Invalid's Wife")

# ABOUT THE AUTHOR

Raised in Vermont's Northeast Kingdom, Jessica Lamb received a master's degree in Italian literature from Stanford University before settling in Portland with her husband, Will, and her son, Hayden. She has taught writing for many years through the Northwest Writing Institute, Portland Community College, and Literary Arts' Writers in the Schools program. Her poems have appeared in numerous journals, including *Poetry*, *The Southern Review*, and *Willow Springs*.

# COLOPHON

Titles are set in Perpetua Tilting Light.
Text is set in Sabon.
Typeset by ImPrint Services, Corvallis, Oregon.